"LOVE ALL, TRUST A FEW, DO WRONG TO NONE"

-WILLIAM SHAKESPEARE

REALITYCOVERBOOKS.COM

I'VE GOT YOUR BACK!

Donald Gorbach

Copyright © 2017 by Donald Gorbach

All rights reserved.

ISBN:1977813844
ISBN-13: 978-1977813848

www.ingramcontent.com/pod-product-compliance
Lightning Source LLC
Chambersburg PA
CBHW050214230526
45470CB00001B/375